Tertullian

De Fuga in Persecutione

Tertullian

De Fuga in Persecutione

Tertullian
De Fuga in Persecutione

Published by
Lighthouse Christian Publishing
SAN 257-4330
5531 Dufferin Drive
Savage, Minnesota, 55378
United States of America

www.lighthousechristianpublishing.com

Tertullian

De Fuga in Persecutione.

1. My brother Fabius, you very lately asked, because some news or other were communicated, whether or not we ought to flee in persecution. For my part, having on the spot made some observations in the negative suited to the place and time, I also, owing to the rudeness of some persons, took away with me the subject but half treated, meaning to set it forth now more fully by my pen; for your inquiry had interested me in it, and the state of the times had already on its own account pressed it upon me. As persecutions in increasing number threaten us, so the more are we called on to give earnest thought to the question of how faith ought to receive them, and the duty of carefully considering it concerns you no less, who no doubt, by not accepting the Comforter, the guide to all truth, have, as was natural, opposed us hitherto in regard to other questions also. We have therefore applied a methodical treatment, too, to your inquiry, as we see that we must first come to a decision as to how the matter stands in regard to persecution itself, whether it comes on us from God or from the devil, that with the less difficulty we may get on firm ground as to our duty to meet it; for of everything one's knowledge is clearer when it is known from whom it has its origin. It is enough indeed to lay it down, (in bar of all besides,) that

nothing happens without the will of God. But lest we be diverted from the point before us, we shall not by this deliverance at once give occasion to the other discussions if one make answer—Therefore evil and sin are both from God; the devil henceforth, and even we ourselves, are entirely free. The question in hand is persecution. With respect to this, let me in the meantime say, that nothing happens without God's will; on the ground that persecution is especially worthy of God, and, so to speak, requisite, for the approving, to wit, or if you will, the rejection of His professing servants. For what is the issue of persecution, what other result comes of it, but the approving and rejecting of faith, in regard to which the Lord will certainly sift His people? Persecution, by means of which one is declared either approved or rejected, is just the judgment of the Lord. But the judging properly belongs to God alone. This is that fan which even now cleanses the Lord's threshing-floor—the Church, I mean—winnowing the mixed heap of believers, and separating the grain of the martyrs from the chaff of the deniers; and this is also the ladder of which Jacob dreams, on which are seen, some mounting up to higher places, and others going down to lower. So, too, persecution may be viewed as a contest. By whom is the conflict proclaimed, but by Him by whom the crown and the rewards are offered? You find in the Revelation its edict, setting forth the rewards by which He incites to victory—those, above all, whose is the distinction of conquering in persecution, in very deed contending in their victorious struggle not against flesh and blood, but against spirits of wickedness. So, too, you will see that the adjudging of the contest belongs to the same glorious One, as umpire, who calls us to the prize. The one great thing in persecution is the promotion of the glory of God, as He tries and casts away, lays on and takes off. But what concerns the glory of God will surely come to pass by His will. And when is trust in God more strong, than when there is a greater fear of Him, and when persecution breaks out? The Church is awe-struck. Then is faith both more zealous in preparation, and better disciplined in fasts, and meetings, and prayers, and lowliness, in brotherly-kindness and love, in holiness and temperance. There is no room, in fact, for ought but fear and hope. So even by this very thing we have it clearly proved that persecution, improving as it does the servants of God, cannot be imputed to the devil.

2. If, because injustice is not from God, but from the devil, and persecution consists of injustice (for what more unjust than that the bishops of the true God, that all the followers of the truth, should be dealt with after the manner of the vilest criminals?), persecution therefore seems to proceed from the devil, by whom the injustice which constitutes persecution is perpetrated, we ought to know, as you have neither persecution without the injustice of the devil, nor the trial of faith without persecution, that the injustice necessary for the trial of faith does not give a warrant for persecution, but supplies an agency; that in reality, in reference to the trial of faith, which is the reason of persecution, the will of God goes first, but that as the instrument of persecution, which is the way of trial, the injustice of the devil follows. For in other respects, too, injustice in proportion to the enmity it displays against righteousness affords occasion for attestations of that to which it is opposed as an enemy, that so righteousness may be perfected in injustice, as strength is perfected in weakness. For the weak things of the world have been chosen by God to confound the strong, and the foolish things of the world to confound its wisdom. Thus even injustice is employed, that righteousness may be approved in putting unrighteousness to shame. Therefore, since the service is not of free-will, but of subjection (for persecution is the appointment of the Lord for the trial of faith, but its ministry is the injustice of the devil, supplied that persecution may be got up), we believe that persecution comes to pass, no question, by the devil's agency, but not by the devil's origination. Satan will not be at liberty to do anything against the servants of the living God unless the Lord grant leave, either that He may overthrow Satan himself

by the faith of the elect which proves victorious in the trial, or in the face of the world show that apostatizers to the devil's cause have been in reality His servants. You have the case of Job, whom the devil, unless he had received authority from God, could not have visited with trial, not even, in fact, in his property, unless the Lord had said, "Behold, all that he has I put at your disposal; but do not stretch out your hand against himself." In short, he would not even have stretched it out, unless afterwards, at his request, the Lord had granted him this permission also, saying, "Behold, I deliver him to you; only preserve his life." So he asked in the case of the apostles likewise an opportunity to tempt them, having it only by special allowance, since the Lord in the Gospel says to Peter, "Behold, Satan asked that he might sift you as grain; but I have prayed for you that your faith fail not;" that is, that the devil should not have power granted him sufficient to endanger
his faith. Whence it is manifest that both things belong to God, the shaking of faith as well as the shielding of it, when both are sought from Him—the shaking by the devil, the shielding by the Son. And certainly, when the Son of God has faith's protection absolutely committed to Him, beseeching it of the Father, from whom He receives all power in heaven and on earth, how entirely out of the question is it that the devil should have the assailing of it in *his* own power! But in the prayer prescribed to us, when we say to our Father, "Lead us not into temptation" (now what greater temptation is there than persecution?), we acknowledge that that comes to pass by His will whom we beseech to exempt us from it. For this is what follows, "But deliver us from the wicked one," that is, do not lead us into temptation by giving us up to the wicked one, for then are we delivered from the power of the devil, when we are not handed over to him to be tempted. Nor would the devil's legion have had power over the herd of swine unless they had got it from God; so far are they from having power over the sheep of God. I may say that the bristles of the swine, too, were then counted by God, not to speak of the hairs of holy men.

The devil, it must be owned, seems indeed to have power—in this case really his own—over those who do not belong to God, the nations being once for all counted by God as a drop of the bucket, and as the dust of the threshing-floor, and as the spittle of the mouth, and so thrown open to the devil as, in a sense, a free possession. But against those who belong to the household of God he may not do ought as by any right of his own, because the cases marked out in Scripture show when—that is, for what reasons—he may touch them. For either, with a view to their being approved, the power of trial is granted to him, challenged or challenging, as in the instances already referred to, or, to secure an opposite result, the sinner is handed over to him, as though he were an executioner to whom belonged the inflicting of punishment, as in the case of Saul. "And the Spirit of the Lord," says Scripture, "departed from Saul, and an evil spirit from the Lord troubled and stifled him;" or the design is to humble, as the apostle tells us, that there was given him a stake, the messenger of Satan, to buffet him; and even this sort of thing is not permitted in the case of holy men, unless it be that at the same time strength of endurance may be perfected in weakness. For the apostle likewise delivered Phygellus and Hermogenes over to Satan that by chastening they might be taught not to blaspheme. You see, then, that the devil receives more suitably power even from the servants of God; so far is he from having it by any right of his own.

3. Seeing therefore, too, these cases occur in persecutions more than at other times, as there is then among us more of proving or rejecting, more of abusing or punishing, it must be that their general occurrence is permitted or commanded by Him at whose will they happen even partially; by Him, I mean, who says, "I am He who make peace and create evil,"—that is, war, for that is the antithesis of peace. But what other war has our peace than persecution? If in its issues persecution emphatically brings either life or death, either wounds or healing, you have the author, too, of this. "I

will smite and heal, I will make alive and put to death." "I will burn them," He says, "as gold is burned; and I will try them," He says, "as silver is tried," for when the flame of persecution is consuming us, then the steadfastness of our faith is proved. These will be the fiery darts of the devil, by which faith gets a ministry of burning and kindling; yet by the will of God. As to this I know not who can doubt, unless it be persons with frivolous and frigid faith, which seizes upon those who with trembling assemble together in the church. For you say, seeing we assemble without order, and assemble at the same time, and flock in large numbers to the church, the heathen are led to make inquiry about us, and we are alarmed lest we awaken their anxieties. Do ye not know that God is Lord of all? And if it is God's will, then you shall suffer persecution; but if it is not, the heathen will be still. Believe it most surely, if indeed you believe in that God without whose will not even the sparrow, a penny can buy, falls to the ground. But we, I think, are better than many sparrows.

4. Well, then, if it is evident from whom persecution proceeds, we are able at once to satisfy your doubts, and to decide from these introductory remarks alone, that men should not flee in it. For if persecution proceeds from God, in no way will it be our duty to flee from what has God as its author; a twofold reason opposing; for what proceeds from God ought not on the one hand to be avoided, and it cannot be evaded on the other. It ought not to be avoided, because it is good; for everything must be good on which God has cast His eye. And with this idea has perhaps this statement been made in Genesis, "And God saw because it is good;" not that He would have been ignorant of its goodness unless He had seen it, but to indicate by this expression that it was good because it was viewed by God. There are many events indeed happening by the will of God, and happening to somebody's harm. Yet for all that, a thing is therefore good because it is of God, as divine, as reasonable; for what is divine, and not reasonable and good? What is good, yet not divine? But if to

the universal apprehension of mankind this seems to be the case, in judging, man's faculty of apprehension does not predetermine the nature of things, but the nature of things his power of apprehension. For every several nature is a certain definite reality, and it lays it on the perceptive power to perceive it just as it exists. Now, if that which comes from God is good indeed in its natural state (for there is nothing from God which is not good, because it is divine, and reasonable), but seems evil only to the human faculty, all will be right in regard to the former; with the latter the fault will lie. In its real nature a very good thing is chastity, and so is truth, and righteousness; and yet they are distasteful to many. Is perhaps the real nature on this account sacrificed to the sense of perception? Thus persecution in its own nature too is good, because it is a divine and reasonable appointment; but those to whom it comes as a punishment do not feel it to be pleasant. You see that as proceeding from Him, even that evil has a reasonable ground, when one in persecution is cast out of a state of salvation, just as you see that you have a reasonable ground for the good also, when one by persecution has his salvation made more secure. Unless, as it depends on the Lord, one either perishes irrationally, or is irrationally saved, he will not be able to speak of persecution as an evil, which, while it is under the direction of reason, is, even in respect of its evil, good. So, if persecution is in every way a good, because it has a natural basis, we on valid grounds lay it down, that what is good ought not to be shunned by us, because it is a sin to refuse what is good; besides that, what has been looked upon by God can no longer indeed be avoided, proceeding as it does from God, from whose will escape will not be possible. Therefore, those who think that they should flee, either reproach God with doing what is evil, if they flee from persecution as an evil (for no one avoids what is good); or they count themselves stronger than God: so they think, who imagine it possible to escape when it is God's pleasure that such events should occur.

5. But, says some one, I flee, the thing it belongs to me to do, that I may not perish, if I deny; it is for Him on His part, if He chooses, to bring me, when I flee, back before the tribunal. First answer me this: Are you sure you will deny if you do not flee, or are you not sure? For if you are sure, you have denied already, because by presupposing that you will deny, you have given yourself up to that about which you have made such a presupposition; and now it is vain for you to think of flight, that you may avoid denying, when in intention you have denied already. But if you are doubtful on that point, why do you not, in the incertitude of your fear wavering between the two different issues, presume that you are able rather to act a confessor's part, and so add to your safety, that you may not flee, just as you presuppose denial to send you off a fugitive? The matter stands thus—we have either both things in our own power, or they wholly lie with God. If it is ours to confess or to deny, why do we not anticipate the nobler thing, that is, that we shall confess? If you are not willing to confess, you are not willing to suffer; and to be unwilling to confess is to deny. But if the matter is wholly in God's hand, why do we not leave it to His will, recognizing His might and power in that, just as He can bring us back to trial when we flee, so is He able to screen us when we do not flee; yes, and even living in the very heart of the people? Strange conduct, is it not, to honor God in the matter of flight from persecution, because He can bring you back from your flight to stand before the judgment-seat; but in regard of witness bearing, to do Him high dishonor by despairing of power at His hands to shield you from danger? Why do you not rather on this, the side of constancy and trust in God, say, I do my part; I depart not; God, if He choose, will Himself be my protector? It beseems us better to retain our position in submission to the will of God, than to flee at our own will. Rutilius, a saintly martyr, after having ofttimes fled from persecution from place to place, nay, having bought security from danger, as he thought, by money, was,

notwithstanding the complete security he had, as he thought, provided for himself, at last unexpectedly seized, and being brought before the magistrate, was put to the torture and cruelly mangled, —a punishment, I believe, for his fleeing, —and thereafter he was consigned to the flames, and thus paid to the mercy of God the suffering which he had shunned. What else did the Lord mean to show us by this example, but that we ought not to flee from persecution because it avails us nothing if God disapproves?

6. Nay, says someone, he fulfilled the command, when he fled from city to city. For so a certain individual, but a fugitive likewise, has chosen to maintain, and others have done the same who are unwilling to understand the meaning of that declaration of the Lord, that they may use it as a cloak for their cowardice, although it has had its persons as well as its times and reasons to which it specially applies. "When they begin," He says, "to persecute you, flee from city to city." We maintain that this belongs specially to the persons of the apostles, and to their times and circumstances, as the following sentences will show, which are suitable only to the apostles: "Do not go into the way of the Gentiles, and into a city of the Samaritans do not enter: but go rather to the lost sheep of the house of Israel." But to us the way of the Gentiles is also open, as in it we in fact were found, and to the very last we walk; and no city has been excepted. So we preach throughout all the world; nay, no special care even for Israel has been laid upon us, save as also we are bound to preach to all nations. Yes, and if we are apprehended, we shall not be brought into Jewish councils, nor scourged in Jewish synagogues, but we shall certainly be cited before Roman magistrates and judgment-seats. So, then, the circumstances of the apostles even required the injunction to flee, their mission being to preach first to the lost sheep of the house of Israel. That, therefore, this preaching might be fully accomplished in the case of those among whom this behooved first of all to be carried out—that the sons might receive bread before the dogs, for that reason He commanded

them to flee then for a time—not with the object of eluding danger, under the plea strictly speaking which persecution urges (rather He was in the habit of proclaiming that they would suffer persecutions, and of teaching that these must be endured); but in order to further the proclamation of the Gospel message, lest by their being at once put down, the diffusion of the Gospel too might be prevented. Neither were they to flee to any city as if by stealth, but as if everywhere about to proclaim their message; and for this, everywhere about to undergo persecutions, until they should fulfil their teaching. Accordingly, the Savior says, "Ye will not go over all the cities of Israel." So the command to flee was restricted to the limits of Judea. But no command that shows Judea to be specially the sphere for preaching applies to us, now that the Holy Spirit has been poured out upon all flesh. Therefore, Paul and the apostles themselves, mindful of the precept of the Lord, bear this solemn testimony before Israel, which they had now filled with their doctrine—saying, "It was necessary that the word of God should have been first delivered to you; but seeing ye have rejected it, and have not thought yourselves worthy of eternal life, lo, we turn to the Gentiles." And from that time they turned their steps away, as those who went before them had laid it down, and departed into the way of the Gentiles, and entered into the cities of the Samaritans; so that, in very deed, their sound went forth into all the earth, and their words to the end of the world. If, therefore, the prohibition against setting foot in the way of the Gentiles, and entering into the cities of the Samaritans, has come to an end, why should not the command to flee, which was issued at the same time, have come also to an end? Accordingly, from the time when, Israel having had its full measure, the apostles went over to the Gentiles, they neither fled from city to city, nor hesitated to suffer. Nay, Paul too, who had submitted to deliverance from persecution by being let down from the wall, as to do so was at this time a matter of command, refused in like manner now at the close of his ministry, and after the injunction had come to an end, to give in to the anxieties of the disciples, eagerly entreating him that he would not risk himself at Jerusalem, because of the sufferings in store for him which Agabus had foretold; but doing the very opposite, it is thus he speaks, "What do ye, weeping and disquieting my heart? For I could wish not only to suffer bonds, but also to die at Jerusalem, for the name of my Lord Jesus Christ." And so they all said, "Let the will of the Lord be done." What was the will of the Lord? Certainly no longer to flee from persecution. Otherwise they who had wished him rather to avoid persecution, might also have adduced that prior will of the Lord, in which He had commanded flight. Therefore, seeing even in the days of the apostles themselves, the command to flee was temporary, as were those also relating to the other things at the same time enjoined, that [command] cannot continue with us which ceased with our teachers, even although it had not been issued specially for them; or if the Lord wished it to continue, the apostles did wrong who were not careful to keep fleeing to the last.

7. Let us now see whether also the rest of our Lord's ordinances accord with a lasting command of flight. In the first place, indeed, if persecution is from God, what are we to think of our being ordered to take ourselves out of its way, by the very party who brings it on us? For if He wanted it to be evaded, He had better not have sent it, that there might not be the appearance of His will being thwarted by another will.

For He wished us either to suffer persecution or to flee from it. If to flee, how to suffer? If to suffer, how to flee? In fact, what utter inconsistency in the decrees of One who commands to flee, and yet urges to suffer, which is the very opposite! "Him who will confess Me, I also will confess before My Father." How will he confess, fleeing? How flee, confessing? "Of him who shall be ashamed of Me, will I also be ashamed before My Father." If I avoid suffering, I am ashamed to confess. "Happy they who suffer persecution for My name's sake." Unhappy, therefore, they who, by running away, will not suffer according to the divine command. "He who shall endure to the end shall be saved." How then, when you bid me flee, do you wish me to endure to the end? If views so opposed to each other do not comport with the divine dignity, they clearly prove that the command to flee had, at the time it was given, a reason of its own, which we have pointed out. But it is said, the Lord, providing for the weakness of some of His people, nevertheless, in His kindness, suggested also the haven of flight to them. For He was not able even without flight—a protection so base, and unworthy, and servile—to preserve in persecution such as He knew to be weak! Whereas in fact He does not cherish, but ever rejects the weak, teaching first, not that we are to fly from our persecutors, but rather that we are not to fear them. "Fear not them who are able to kill the body, but are unable to do ought against the soul; but fear Him who can destroy both body and soul in hell." And then what does He allot to the fearful? "He who will value his life more than Me, is not worthy of Me; and he who takes not up his cross and follows Me, cannot be My disciple." Last of all, in the Revelation, He does not propose flight to the "fearful," but a miserable portion among the rest of the outcast, in the lake of brimstone and fire, which is the second death.

8. He sometimes also fled from violence Himself, but for the same reason as had led Him to command the apostles to do so: that is, He wanted to fulfil His ministry of teaching; and when it was finished, I do not say He stood firm, but He had no desire even to get from His Father the aid of hosts of angels: finding fault, too, with Peter's sword. He likewise acknowledged, it is true, that His "soul was troubled, even unto death," and the flesh weak; with the design, (however,) first of all, that by having, as His own, trouble of soul and weakness of the flesh, He might show you that both the substances in Him were truly human; lest, as certain persons have now brought it in, you might be led to think either the flesh or the soul of Christ different from ours; and then, that, by an exhibition of their states, you might be convinced that they have no power at

all of themselves without the spirit. And for this reason He puts first "the willing spirit," that, looking to the natures respectively of both the substances, you may see that you have in you the spirit's strength as well as the flesh's weakness; and even from this may learn what to do, and by what means to do it, and what to bring under what, —the weak, namely, under the strong, that you may not, as is now your fashion, make excuses on the ground of the weakness of the flesh, forsooth, but put
out of sight the strength of the spirit. He also asked of His Father, that if it might be, the cup of suffering should pass from Him. So ask you the like favor; but as He did, holding your position, —merely offering supplication, and adding, too, the other words: "but not what I will, but what Thou wilt." But when you run away, how will you make this request? taking, in that case, into your own hands the removal of the cup from you, and instead of doing what your Father wishes, doing what you wish yourself.

9. The teaching of the apostles was surely in everything according to the mind of God: they forgot and omitted nothing of the Gospel. Where, then, do you show that they renewed the command to flee from city to city? In fact, it was utterly impossible that they should have laid down anything so utterly opposed to their own examples as a command to flee, while it was just from bonds, or the islands in which, for confessing, not fleeing from the Christian name, they were confined, they wrote their letters to the Churches. Paul bids us support the weak, but most certainly it is not when they flee. For how can the absent be supported by you? By bearing with them? Well, he says that people must be supported, if anywhere they have committed a fault through the weakness of their faith, just as (he enjoins) that we should comfort the faint-hearted; he does not say, however, that they should be sent into exile. But when he urges us not to give place to evil, he does not offer the suggestion that we should take to our heels, he only teaches that passion should be kept

under restraint; and if he says that the time must be redeemed, because the days are evil, he wishes us to gain a lengthening of life, not by flight, but by wisdom. Besides, he who bids us shine as sons of light, does not bid us hide away out of sight as sons of darkness. He commands us to stand steadfast, certainly not to act an opposite part by fleeing; and to be girt, not to play the fugitive or oppose the Gospel. He points out weapons, too, which persons who intend to run away would not require. And among these he notes the shield too, that ye may be able to quench the darts of the devil, when doubtless ye resist him, and sustain his assaults in their utmost force. Accordingly, John also teaches that we must lay down our lives for the brethren; much more, then, we must do it for the Lord. This cannot be fulfilled by those who flee. Finally, mindful of his own Revelation, in which he had heard the doom of the fearful, (and so) speaking from personal knowledge, he warns us that fear must be put away. "There is no fear," says he, "in love; but perfect love casteth out fear; because fear has torment"—the fire of the lake, no doubt. "He that feareth is not perfect in love"—to wit, the love of God. And yet who will flee from persecution, but he who fears? Who will fear, but he who has not loved? Yes; and if you ask counsel of the Spirit, what does He approve more than that utterance of the Spirit? For, indeed, it incites all almost to go and offer themselves in martyrdom, not to flee from it; so that we also make mention of it. If you are exposed to public infamy, says he, it is for your good; for he who is not exposed to dishonor among men is sure to be so before the Lord. Do not be ashamed; righteousness brings you forth into the public gaze. Why should you be ashamed of gaining glory? The opportunity is given you when you are before the eyes of men. So also elsewhere: seek not to die on bridal beds, nor in miscarriages, nor in soft fevers, but to die the martyr's death, that He may be glorified who has suffered for you.

10. But some, paying no attention to the exhortations of God, are readier to apply to themselves that Greek versicle of worldly wisdom, “He who fled will fight again;” perhaps also in the battle to flee again. And when will he who, as a fugitive, is a defeated man, be conqueror? A worthy soldier he furnishes to his commander Christ, who, so amply armed by the apostle, as soon as he hears persecution’s trumpet, runs off from the day of persecution. I also will produce in answer a quotation taken from the world: “Is it a thing so very sad to die?” He must die, in whatever way of it, either as conquered or as conqueror. But although he has succumbed in denying, he has yet faced and battled with the torture. I had rather be one to be pitied than to be blushed for. More glorious is the soldier pierced with a javelin in battle, than he who has a safe skin as a fugitive. Do you fear man, O Christian? —you who ought to be feared by the angels, since you are to judge angels; who ought to be feared by evil spirits, since you have received power also over evil spirits; who ought to be feared by the whole world, since by you, too, the world is judged. You are Christ clothed, you who flee before the devil, since into Christ you have been baptized. Christ, who is in you, is treated as of small account when you give yourself back to the devil, by becoming a fugitive before him. But, seeing it is from the Lord you flee, you taunt all runaways with the futility of their purpose. A certain bold prophet also had fled from the Lord, he had crossed over from Joppa in the direction of Tarsus, as if he could as easily transport himself away from God; but I find him, I do not say in the sea and on the land, but, in fact, in the belly even of a beast, in which he was confined for the space of three days, unable either to find death or even thus escape from God. How much better the conduct of the man who, though he fears the enemy of God, does not flee from, but rather despises him, relying on the protection of the Lord; or, if you will, having an awe of God all the greater, the more that he has stood in His presence, says, “It is the Lord, He is mighty. All things belong to Him; wherever I am, I am in

His hand: let Him do as He wills, I go not away; and if it be His pleasure that I die, let Him destroy me Himself, while I save myself for Him. I had rather bring odium upon Him by dying by His will, than by escaping through my own anger."

11. Thus ought every servant of God to feel and act, even one in an inferior place, that he may come to have a more important one, if he has made some upward step by his endurance of persecution. But when persons in authority themselves—I mean the very deacons, and presbyters, and bishops—take to flight, how will a layman be able to see with what view it was said, Flee from city to city? Thus, too, with the leaders turning their backs, who of the common rank will hope to persuade men to stand firm in the battle? Most assuredly a good shepherd lays down his life for the sheep, according to the word of Moses, when the Lord Christ had not as yet been revealed, but was already shadowed forth in himself: "If you destroy this people," he says, "destroy me also along with it." But Christ, confirming these foreshadowings Himself, adds: "The bad shepherd is he who, on seeing the wolf, flees, and leaves the sheep to be torn in pieces." Why, a shepherd like this will be turned off from the farm; the wages to have been given him at the time of his discharge will be kept from him as compensation; nay, even from his former savings a restoration of the master's loss will be required; for "to him who hath shall be given, but from him who hath not shall be taken away even that which he seemeth to have." Thus Zechariah threatens: "Arise, O sword, against the shepherds, and pluck ye out the sheep; and I will turn my hand against the shepherds." And against them both Ezekiel and Jeremiah declaim with kindred threatenings, for their not only wickedly eating of the Sheep, —they feeding themselves rather than those committed to their charge, —but also scattering the flock, and giving it over, shepherdless, a prey to all the beasts of the field. And this never happens more than when in persecution the Church is abandoned by the clergy. If anyone recognizes

the Spirit also, he will hear him branding the runaways. But if it does not become the keepers of the flock to flee when the wolves invade it—nay, if that is absolutely unlawful (for He who has declared a shepherd of this sort a bad one has certainly condemned him; and whatever is condemned has, without doubt, become unlawful)—on this ground it will not be the duty of those who have been set over the Church to flee in the time of persecution. But otherwise, if the flock should flee, the overseer of the flock would have no call to hold his ground, as his doing so in that case would be, without good reason, to give to the flock protection, which it would not require in consequence of its liberty, forsooth, to flee.

12. So far, my brother, as the question proposed by you is concerned, you have our opinion in answer and encouragement. But he who inquires whether persecution ought to be shunned by us must now be prepared to consider the following question also: Whether, if we should not flee from it, we should at least buy ourselves off from it. Going further than you expected, therefore, I will also on this point give you my advice, distinctly affirming that persecution, from which it is evident we must not flee, must in like manner not even be bought off. The difference lies in the payment; but as flight is a buying off without money, so buying off is money-flight. Assuredly you have here too the counselling of fear. Because you fear, you buy yourself off; and so you flee. As regards your feet, you have stood; in respect of the money you have paid, you have run away. Why, in this very standing of yours there was a fleeing from persecution, in the release from persecution which you bought; but that you should ransom with money a man whom Christ has ransomed with His blood, how unworthy is it of God and His ways of acting, who spared not His own Son for you, that He might be made a curse for us, because cursed is he that hangeth on a tree, —Him who was led as a sheep to be a sacrifice, and just as a lamb before its shearer, so opened He not His mouth; but gave His back to the scourges, nay, His cheeks to the hands of the smiter, and

turned not away His face from spitting, and, being numbered with the transgressors, was delivered up to death, nay, the death of the cross. All this took place that He might redeem us from our sins. The sun ceded to us the day of our redemption; hell re-transferred the right it had in us, and our covenant is in heaven; the everlasting gates were lifted up, that the King of Glory, the Lord of might, might enter in, after having redeemed man from earth, nay, from hell, that he might attain to heaven. What, now, are we to think of the man who strives against that glorious One, nay, slights and defiles His goods, obtained at so great a ransom—no less, in truth, than His most precious blood? It appears, then, that it is better to flee than to fall in value, if a man will not lay out for himself as much as he cost Christ. And the Lord indeed ransomed him from the angelic powers which rule the world—from the spirits of wickedness, from the darkness of this life, from eternal judgment, from everlasting death. But *you* bargain for him with an informer, or a soldier or some paltry thief of a ruler—under, as they say, the folds of the tunic—as if *he* were stolen goods whom Christ purchased in the face of the whole world, yes, and set at liberty. Will you value, then, this free man at any price, and possess him at any price, but the one, as we have said, it cost the Lord, —namely, His own blood? (And if not,) why then do you purchase Christ in the man in whom He dwells, as though He were some human property? No otherwise did Simon even try to do, when he offered the apostles money for the Spirit of Christ. Therefore, this man also, who in buying himself has bought the Spirit of Christ, will hear that word, “Your money perishes with you, since you have thought that the grace of God is to be had at a price!” Yet who will despise him for being (what he is), a denier? For what says that extorter? Give me money: assuredly that he may not deliver him up, since he tries to sell you nothing else than that which he is going to give you for money. When you put that into his hands, it is certainly your wish *not* to be delivered up. But not delivered up, had you to be held up to public ridicule? While, then, in being unwilling to be delivered up, you are not willing to be thus exposed; by this unwillingness of yours you have denied that you are what you have been unwilling to have it made public that you are. Nay, you say, While I am unwilling to be held up to the public as being what I am, I have acknowledged that I am what I am unwilling to be so held up as being, that is, a Christian. Can Christ, therefore, claim that you, as a witness for Him, have steadfastly shown Him forth? He who buys himself off does nothing in that way. Before *one* it might, I doubt not, be said, You have confessed Him; so also, on the account of your unwillingness to confess Him before many you have denied Him. A man's very safety will pronounce that he has fallen while getting out of persecution's way. He has fallen, therefore, whose desire has been to escape. The refusal of martyrdom is denial. A Christian is preserved by his wealth, and for this end has his treasures, that he may not suffer, while he will be rich toward God. But it is the case that Christ was rich in blood for him. Blessed therefore are the poor, because, He says, the kingdom of heaven is theirs who have the soul only treasured up. If we cannot serve God and mammon, can we be redeemed both by God and by mammon? For who will serve mammon more than the man whom mammon has ransomed? Finally, of what example do you avail yourself to warrant your averting by money the giving of you up? When did the apostles, dealing with the matter, in any time of persecution trouble, extricate themselves by money? And money they certainly had from the prices of lands which were laid down at their feet, there being, without a doubt, many of the rich among those who believed—men, and also women, who were wont, too, to minister to their comfort. When did Onesimus, or Aquila, or Stephen, give them aid of this kind when they were persecuted? Paul indeed, when Felix the governor hoped that he should receive money for him from the disciples, about which matter he also dealt with the apostle in private, certainly neither paid it himself, nor did the disciples for him. Those disciples, at any rate, who wept because he was equally persistent in his determination to go to Jerusalem, and neglectful of all means to secure himself from the persecutions which had been foretold as about to occur there, at last say, "Let the will of the Lord be done." What was that will? No doubt that he should suffer for the name of the Lord, not that he should be bought off. For as Christ laid down His life for us, so, too, we should do for Him; and not only for the Lord Himself, nay, but likewise for our brethren on His account. This, too, is the teaching of John when he declares, not that we should pay for our brethren, but rather that we should die for them. It makes no difference whether the thing not to be done by you is to buy *off* a Christian, or to *buy* one. And so the will of God accords with this. Look at the condition—certainly of God's ordaining, in whose hand the king's heart is—of kingdoms and empires. For increasing the treasury there are daily provided so many appliances—registerings of property, taxes in kind benevolences, taxes in money; but never up to this time has ought of the kind been provided by bringing Christians under some purchase-money for the person and the sect, although enormous gains could be reaped from numbers too great for any to be ignorant of them. Bought with blood, paid for with blood, we owe no money for our head, because Christ is our Head. It is not fit that Christ should cost us money. How could martyrdoms, too, take place to the glory of the Lord, if by tribute we should pay for the liberty of our sect? And so he who stipulates to have it at a price, opposes the divine appointment. Since, therefore, Cæsar has imposed nothing on us after this fashion of a tributary sect—in fact, such an imposition never can be made, —with Antichrist now close at hand, and gaping for the blood, not for the money of Christians—how can it be pointed out to me that there is the command, "Render to Cæsar the things which are Cæsar's?" A soldier, be he an informer or an enemy, extorts money from me by threats, exacting nothing on Cæsar's behalf; nay, doing the very opposite, when for a bribe he lets me go—Christian as I am, and by the laws of man a criminal. Of another sort is the *denarius* which I owe to Cæsar, a thing belonging to him, about which the question then was started, it being a tribute coin due indeed by those subject to tribute, not by children. Or how shall I render to God the things which are God's, —certainly, therefore, His own likeness and money inscribed with His name, that is, a Christian man? But what do I owe God, as I do Cæsar the *denarius*, but the blood which His own Son shed for me? Now if I owe God, indeed, a human being and my own blood; but I am now in this juncture, that a demand is made upon me for the payment of that debt, I am undoubtedly guilty of cheating God if I do my best to withhold payment. I have well kept the commandment, if, rendering to Cæsar the things which are Cæsar's, I refuse to God the things which are God's!

13. But also to everyone who asks me I will give on the plea of charity, not under any intimidation. Who asks? He says. But he who uses intimidation does not ask. One who threatens if he does not receive, does not crave, but compels. It is not alms he looks for, who comes not to be pitied, but to be feared. I will give, therefore, because I pity, not because I fear, when the recipient honors God and returns me his blessing; not when rather he both believes that he has conferred a favor on me, and, beholding his plunder, says, "Guilt money." Shall I be angry even with an enemy? But enmities have also other grounds. Yet withal he did not say a betrayer, or persecutor, or one seeking to terrify you by his threats. For how much more shall I heap coals upon the head of a man of this sort, if I do not redeem myself by money? "In like manner," says Jesus, "to him who has taken away your coat, grant even your cloak also." But that refers to him who has sought to take away my property, not my faith. The cloak, too, I will grant, if I am not threatened with betrayal. If he threatens, I will demand even my coat back again. Even now, the declarations of the Lord have reasons and laws of their own. They are not of unlimited or universal application. And so He commands us to give to everyone who asks, yet He Himself does not give to

those who ask a sign. Otherwise, if you think that we should give indiscriminately to all who ask, that seems to me to mean that you would give, I say not wine to him who has a fever, but even poison or a sword to him who longs for death. But how we are to understand, "Make to yourselves friends of mammon," let the previous parable teach you. The saying was addressed to the Jewish people; inasmuch as, having managed ill the business of the Lord which had been entrusted to them, they ought to have provided for themselves out of the men of mammon, which we then were, friends rather than enemies, and to have delivered us from the dues of sins which kept us from God, if they bestowed the blessing upon us, for the reason given by the Lord, that when grace began to depart from them, they, betaking themselves to our faith, might be admitted into everlasting habitations. Hold now any other explanation of this parable and saying you like, if only you clearly see that there is no likelihood of our opposers, should we make them friends with mammon, then receiving us into everlasting abodes. But of what will not cowardice convince men? As if Scripture both allowed them to flee, and commanded them to buy off! Finally, it is not enough if one or another is so rescued. Whole Churches have imposed tribute *en masse* on themselves. I know not whether it is matter for grief or shame when among hucksters, and pickpockets, and bath-thieves, and gamesters, and pimps, Christians too are included as taxpayers in the lists of free soldiers and spies. Did the apostles, with so much foresight, make the office of overseer of this type, that the occupants might be able to enjoy their rule free from anxiety, under color of providing (a like freedom for their flocks)? For such a peace, forsooth, Christ, returning to His Father, commanded to be bought from the soldiers by gifts like those you have in the Saturnalia!

14. But how shall we assemble together? say you; how shall we observe the ordinances of the Lord? To be sure, just as the apostles also did, who were protected by faith, not by money; which faith, if it can remove a mountain, can much

more remove a soldier. Be your safeguard wisdom, not a bribe. For you will not have at once complete security from the people also, should you buy off the interference of the soldiers. Therefore, all you need for your protection is to have both faith and wisdom: if you do not make use of these, you may lose even the deliverance which you have purchased for yourself; while, if you do employ them, you can have no need of any ransoming. Lastly, if you cannot assemble by day, you have the night, the light of Christ luminous against its darkness. You cannot run about among them one after another. Be content with a church of threes. It is better that you sometimes should not see your crowds, than subject yourselves (to a tribute bondage). Keep pure for Christ His betrothed virgin; let no one make gain of her. These things, my brother, seem to you perhaps harsh and not to be endured; but recall that God has said, "He who receives it, let him receive it," that is, let him who does not receive it go his way. He who fears to suffer, cannot belong to Him who suffered. But the man who does not fear to suffer, he will be perfect in love—in the love, it is meant, of God; "for perfect love casteth out fear." "And therefore many are called, but few chosen." It is not asked who is ready to follow the broad way, but who the narrow. And therefore the Comforter is requisite, who guides into all truth, and animates to all endurance. And they who have received Him will neither stoop to flee from persecution nor to buy it off, for they have the Lord Himself, One who will stand by us to aid us in suffering, as well as to be our mouth when we are put to the question.

Elucidations.

I.

(Persecutions threaten, p. 116.)

We have reserved this heroic tract to close our series of the ascetic essays of our author because it places even his sophistical enthusiasm in a light which shows much to admire. Strange that this defiant hero should have died (as we may infer) in his bed, and in extreme old age. Great man, how much, alike for weal and woe, the ages have been taught by thee!

This is the place for a tabular view of the *ten persecutions* of the Ante-Nicene Church.
They are commonly enumerated as follows: —

1. Under Nero——a.d. 64.
2. Under Trajan——a.d. 95.
3. Under Trajan——a.d. 107.
4. Under Hadrian (a.d. 118 and) ——a.d. 134.
5. Under Aurelius (a.d. 177) and Severus——a.d. 202.
6. Under Maximin——a.d. 235.
7. Under Decius——a.d. 250.
8. Under Valerian——a.d. 254.
9. Under Aurelian——a.d. 270.
10. Under Diocletian (a.d. 284 and) ——a.d. 303.

Periods of Comparative Rest.

1. Under Antoninus Pius——a.d. 151.
2. Under Commodus——a.d. 185.
3. Under Alexander Severus——a.d. 223.
4. Under Philip——a.d. 248.
5. Under Diocletian——a.d. 284 till a.d. 303.

In thus chastising and sifting his Church in the years of her gradual growth "from the smallest of all seeds," we see illustrations of the Lord's Epistles to the seven churches of the Apocalypse. Who can doubt that Tertullian's writings prepared the North-African Church for the Decian furnace, and all believers for the "seven times hotter" fires of Diocletian?

II.

(To the fearful, p. 120.)

In the *Patientia* Tertullian reflects the views of Catholics, and seems to allow those "persecuted in one city to flee to another." So also in the *Ad Uxorem*, as instanced by Kaye. In the *Fuga* we have the enthusiast, but not as Gibbon will have it, the most wild and fanatical of declaimers. On the whole subject we again refer our readers to the solid and sober comments of Kaye on the martyrdoms and persecutions of the early faithful, and on the patristic views of the same.

III.

(Enormous gains from numbers, p. 124.)

Christians were now counted by millions. The following tabular view of the Christian population of the world from the beginning has been attributed to *Sharon Turner*. I do not find it in any of his works with which I am familiar. The *nineteenth century* is certainly credited too low, according to the modern computists; but I insert it merely for the centuries we are now considering.

Growth of the Church in Numbers.

1. First century——500,000

2. Second century——2,000,000
3. Third century——5,000,000
4. Fourth century——10,000,000
5. Fifth century——15,000,000
6. Sixth century——20,000,000
7. Seventh century——24,000,000
8. Eighth century——30,000,000
9. Ninth century——40,000,000
10. Tenth century——50,000,000
11. Eleventh century——70,000,000
12. Twelfth century——80,000,000
13. Thirteenth century——75,000,000
14. Fourteenth century——80,000,000
15. Fifteenth century——100,000,000
16. Sixteenth century——125,000,000
17. Seventeenth century——155,000,000
18. Eighteenth century——200,000,000
19. Nineteenth century——400,000,000

www.ingramcontent.com/pod-product-compliance
Lightning Source LLC
Chambersburg PA
CBHW071015120726
47910CB00004B/1528

9781643730929